Contents

Introduction
to Course & Subjects

Course Outline

This is a four part course designed to help participants learn more about their faith and how to apply it to everyday life, how to study the Bible, explore theology and become more effective leaders.

The subjects and some of the elements covered are:

Bible: Jesus, The Bible & You –
* How to read the Bible devotionally and for study purposes
* Historical background to the Bible
* How to use all the Bible study tools
* How to get revelations from the Bible

Leadership: The Church & Your Leadership Journey – Learn effective leadership qualities and skills that can build your own life and the lives of others, seeing the kingdom of God move forward.

Lifestyle: Following Jesus –
* How to build a strong devotional life
* How to find your purpose in God
* How to live a life that can fulfil your purpose
* How to hear from God

Theology: Faith Foundations – Develop a personal theology in a biblical and thoughtful way that will be a blessing to you and your church community.

Learning Sessions

Once per week for 2½ hours which includes 2 teaching sessions, 1 application session and a 20min break (after session 1).

Teaching Sessions – each week will include 2 x 50 minute sessions in a lecture style.

Application Sessions – each week will consist of 1 x 25 minute group session where homework and previous teaching
sessions will be used to stimulate discussion. These sessions will vary in activities including multimedia and role playing etc.

Homework

Each week you will get a small amount of work to complete at home. It should take about 20 minutes to complete and it will be used to stimulate discussion the following week during the group session. There are also some advanced questions for those who wish to do more in-depth study.

Bible Version

Throughout this course the New International Version (NIV) has been used unless otherwise specified.

Many translations can be viewed freely from websites such as: **www.biblegateway.com**, **www. biblestudytools.com** and
www.bible.cc or on your mobile device using applications such as **YouVersion**. We encourage you to research and find what works best for you.

Before you commence spend a few moments to pray and ask the Holy Spirit to give you eyes to see what the Word is saying to you.

Lifestyle
Following Jesus

This subject gives a seven week overview of how to develop a strong devotional life with God; finding your purpose and fulfilment in Him.

Recommend Reading

If you want to get a deeper understanding of this subject, here are some recommended resources.

✱ Edwards, Mark, **One Day Over A Coffee**, (Ipswich Region Community Church: Toowoomba, 2007)

✱ Foster, Richard, **Celebration of Discipline**, (Hodder & Stoughton: London, 2008)

✱ Houston, Brian, **For This I Was Born**, (Thomas Nelson, Nashville, 2008)

✱ Houston, Brian, **The Maximised Life Series**, (Maximised Leadership, Sydney)

✱ MacDonald, Gordon, **Ordering Your Private World**, (International Press, New York, 1985)

✱ Meyer, Joyce, **Battlefield of the mind**, (Faith Words, New York, 1995)

✱ Warren, Rick, **The Purpose Driven Life**, (Zondervan, Michigan, 2002)

Week¹

Introduction

Session 1 –
Introduction to Lifestyle

The Christian Lifestyle
Jesus is Our Example

Break

Session 2 –
Building a Relationship with God:
Devotional Bible Reading and Journaling

Reading the Bible Devotionally
Journaling

Session 3 –
SOAP Journaling Exercise

Homework –
Our Church's Lifestyle
SOAP Journal

Session 1
Introduction to Lifestyle

Outcomes

By the end of this session, you will be able to:
* Explain the Christian way of life and why it is important
* Describe what it means to follow Christ's example

The Christian Lifestyle

Jesus is Our Example

Session 2
Building a Relationship with God: Devotional Bible Study and Journaling

Outcomes

By the end of this session, you will be able to:
* Understand the importance of devotional Bible study
* Read the Bible devotionally
* Record and process their devotional life through journaling

Reading the Bible Devotionally

_____
_____
_____
_____
_____
_____
_____
_____
_____
_____
_____
_____
_____
_____
_____
_____
_____
_____
_____
_____
_____
_____
_____

Journaling

Session 3
SOAP Journaling Exercise

The best way to get the greatest blessing out of your devotional reading is to journal what God is saying to you through the passage. We encourage you to use the SOAP method of journaling. The acronym SOAP stands for Scripture, Observation, Application and Prayer.

Before you start, pray and ask the Holy Spirit to open your eyes to see and ears to listen; to give you insight into the passage that you will read.

Read John 13:1-17. Spend a few minutes thinking about what the text means. Ask yourself, "Which particular passage do I find striking?"

_____

_____

_____

_____

_____

_____

_____

_____

_____

_____

_____

_____

_____

_____

_____

_____

_____

_____

Jot down your observations or impressions. Re-read the passage that you find striking. Ask yourself, "What is the Lord saying to me in this passage with regard to my life?"

_____

_____

_____

_____

_____

_____

_____

_____

_____

_____

If you have a particular need, ask yourself, "How does this passage apply to my particular need?"

_____

_____

_____

_____

_____

_____

_____

_____

_____

_____

_____

Application. Ask yourself, "How will I respond to what God has revealed to me?"

_____

_____

_____

_____

_____

_____

_____

_____

_____

_____

_____

Pray. You can also write your prayer. It doesn't have to be long.

_____

_____

_____

_____

_____

_____

_____

_____

_____

_____

_____

_____

_____

Homework

Embracing my church's way of life

Describe what you believe is the kind of lifestyle your local church is encouraging you to live.

_____

_____

_____

_____

_____

_____

_____

_____

_____

_____

_____

_____

_____

_____

_____

_____

_____

_____

_____

_____

_____

_____

_____

_____

_____

_____

How is the lifestyle being demonstrated by your local church?

In what ways is such a lifestyle being demonstrated in your life?

_____

_____

_____

_____

_____

_____

_____

_____

_____

_____

_____

_____

_____

_____

_____

_____

_____

_____

_____

_____

_____

_____

_____

_____

_____

_____

_____

SOAP Journal

Consistency is critical if we want to deepen our relationship with God on a daily basis. We therefore encourage you to regularly do the Devotional Reading and Journaling Exercise throughout the course.

For this week, read **Luke 11:1-5** and reflect on the passage. Always ask the Holy Spirit to give you insight and to open the Word to you.

Read: _____

Which particular passage did I find striking?

_____

_____

_____

_____

_____

_____

What is the Lord saying to me in this passage with regard to my life?

_____

_____

_____

_____

_____

_____

_____

_____

_____

_____

_____

_____

_____

_____

How does this passage apply to my particular need?

_____

_____

_____

_____

_____

_____

_____

How will I respond to what God has revealed to me?

_____

_____

_____

_____

_____

_____

_____

_____

My prayer:

_____

_____

_____

_____

_____

_____

_____

_____

_____

Week²

Introduction

Session 1 –
Building a Relationship with God: Prayer

What is Prayer?
Types of Prayer
Developing a Prayer Life

Break

Session 2 –
Building a Relationship with God:
Hearing God's Voice and Being Led by the Spirit

Hearing God's Voice
Filtering Out the Voices that are not God's

Session 3 –
Hearing God's Voice through Prayer

Homework –
Listening to the Shepherd's Voice
SOAP Journal

Session 1
Building a Relationship with God: Prayer

Outcomes

By the end of this session, you will be able to:
* Understand the importance of prayer
* Identify different types of prayer
* Describe keys to developing a personal prayer life

What is Prayer?

_____

_____

_____

_____

_____

_____

_____

_____

_____

_____

_____

_____

_____

_____

_____

_____

_____

_____

_____

_____

_____

Types of Prayer

Developing a Prayer Life

Session 2

Building a Relationship with God: Hearing God's Voice and Being Led by the Spirit

Outcomes

By the end of this session, you will be able to:

★ Understand that God speaks in various ways and apply what has been learned

★ Recognise the need for discernment when being led by the Spirit

Hearing God's Voice

_____

_____

_____

_____

_____

_____

_____

_____

_____

_____

_____

_____

_____

_____

_____

_____

_____

_____

_____

_____

_____

Filtering Out the Voices that are not God's

Session 3
Hearing God's voice through prayer

Jesus tells us in John 8:47 that, "He who belongs to God hears what God says." This means that the ability to hear God's voice is not just for prophets but for all believers.

One way that we can hear God's voice is through our prayer. Unfortunately, we often do all the talking and do not take time to stop, wait and listen to what God will say. But when we do, the experience is life changing.

Share an experience when you heard the voice of God in your prayer.

How did you know that it was the voice of God and not your own?

_____

_____

_____

_____

_____

_____

_____

_____

_____

_____

What did you do when you heard the voice of God?

_____

_____

_____

_____

_____

_____

_____

_____

_____

What effect did the experience have on you?

_____

_____

_____

_____

_____

_____

_____

_____

_____

_____

_____

_____

_____

_____

_____

_____

_____

_____

_____

_____

_____

_____

_____

_____

_____

_____

_____

_____

_____

What hindrances to hearing God's voice did you have to overcome?

What do you need to do to create an atmosphere where you can regularly hear the voice of God and be sensitive to the leading of the Holy Spirit?

Homework

Read John 10:1-18.

What can we learn from the text in terms of how we should respond to the presence of God?

_____

_____

_____

_____

_____

_____

_____

_____

_____

_____

What do you think are the reasons why the sheep was able to recognise the voice of the Shepherd?

_____

_____

_____

_____

_____

_____

_____

_____

_____

_____

_____

_____

What assurance does it give you to know that the Shepherd promises to lead His sheep?

_____

_____

_____

_____

_____

_____

_____

_____

_____

_____

_____

_____

_____

_____

_____

_____

_____

_____

_____

_____

_____

_____

_____

_____

_____

What can you learn about the relationship between the sheep and the Shepherd?

_____

_____

_____

_____

_____

_____

_____

_____

_____

_____

_____

_____

_____

_____

_____

_____

_____

_____

_____

_____

_____

_____

_____

_____

_____

_____

_____

How would you suggest that a new believer grow to recognise His voice?

SOAP Journal

Consistency is critical if we want to deepen our relationship with God on a daily basis. We therefore encourage you to regularly do the SOAP Exercise throughout the course.

For this week read **Luke 11:9-13**. Always ask the Holy Spirit to give you insight and to open the Word to you.

Which particular passage did I find striking?

_____

_____

_____

_____

_____

_____

_____

What is the Lord saying to me in this passage with regard to my life?

_____

_____

_____

_____

_____

_____

_____

_____

_____

_____

_____

_____

_____

_____

_____

How does this passage apply to my particular need?

_____

_____

_____

_____

_____

_____

How will I respond to what God has revealed to me?

_____

_____

_____

_____

_____

_____

_____

My prayer:

_____

_____

_____

_____

_____

_____

_____

_____

_____

_____

As you apply during the week what God has said to you, keep your ears open to whatever else God will say to you about the matter. You'll be pleasantly surprised, He has more!

Week³

Introduction

**Session 1 –
Building a Relationship with God:
Growing in Faith**

The Importance of Faith
The Nature of Faith
Walking in Faith

Break

**Session 2 –
Building a Relationship with God:
Worship, Personal and Corporate**

Worship as a Lifestyle
Worship, Personal and Corporate

**Session 3 –
Living by Faith**

**Homework –
Serving as Worship
SOAP Journal**

Session 1

Building a Relationship with God: Growing in Faith

Outcomes

By the end of this session, you will be able to:
* Appreciate the importance of faith in their walk with God
* Understand the nature of faith, the role that the Bible plays and different types of faith
* Recognise ways in which they can grow in faith and live a lifestyle of faith

The Importance of Faith

The Nature of Faith

Walking in Faith

Session 2

Building a Relationship with God :
Worship, Personal and Corporate

Outcomes

By the end of this session, you will be able to:
* Describe and differentiate between various definitions of worship
* Explain the power and place of worship in the Christian's walk with God
* Explain the difference between personal and corporate worship

Worship as a Lifestyle

Personal and Corporate Worship

Session 3
Living by Faith

Christians are called to live by faith, to stand in faith and to walk in faith (Galatians 2:20; Romans 11:20; 2 Corinthians 1:24; Romans 4:12; 2 Corinthians 5:7).

In your small group, discuss the following questions:

What does it personally mean to you to live, stand and walk by faith?

_____

_____

_____

_____

_____

_____

_____

_____

_____

_____

What kind of a faith picture do you have for your life, family, marriage, job or your business?

_____

_____

_____

_____

_____

_____

_____

_____

_____

_____

What would happen if belief and faith are strongly entrenched in your life?

_____

_____

_____

_____

_____

_____

_____

_____

_____

_____

_____

_____

Will there be any difference in the way you will live your life? What will be the difference?

_____

_____

_____

_____

_____

_____

_____

_____

_____

_____

_____

_____

_____

_____

_____

How do you remain a person of faith when everything around you speaks of unbelief and doubt?

_____

_____

_____

_____

_____

_____

_____

_____

_____

What practical steps will you take to enable you to develop your faith?

_____

_____

_____

_____

_____

_____

_____

_____

_____

_____

Faith Exercise

List your faith declarations. These may include promises that God has given you, what you see God is doing in all areas of your life and what you desire to see God do in your life. To help you align your faith declarations to the Word of God, find a verse or two that affirms it. In the next seven days, declare (speak out loud) your faith declarations and open your heart to what God is going to do in you!

Homework

Serving as Worship

Worship is a way of life. It is not something that we do but rather who we are. As such, we cannot separate our individual worship from our corporate worship. Neither can we substitute one for the other as both are vital to our health as a believer and the body of Christ.

Read Romans 12:1-2. Often defined as adoration, Paul in this verse gives us another meaning of worship, which is to serve, work or minister. Keeping this definition in mind, answer the following questions:

What does the phrase 'present our bodies as a living sacrifice' mean to you?

_____

_____

_____

_____

_____

_____

_____

_____

_____

_____

_____

_____

Describe a situation when you have placed your entire self at God's disposal. What was the result of that experience?

_____

_____

_____

_____

_____

_____

_____

_____

Do you hold back in terms of your physical energy, your material resources, or your time in serving God? What do you need to do to present to God on a consistent basis your entire self and not just a part of yourself?

_____

_____

_____

_____

_____

_____

_____

_____

_____

_____

What are the implications of offering our lives to God as a sacrifice (v2)?

_____

_____

_____

_____

_____

_____

_____

_____

_____

_____

_____

_____

How will you practically apply this learning of worship as service in your local church?

_____

_____

_____

_____

_____

_____

_____

_____

_____

_____

_____

Optional Homework

Create a list of adjectives that describe God and use them in your personal worship towards Him. A good place to start in creating your list is the Book of Psalms.

Pray through one of the more exultant psalms, or some of the worship passages in Revelation.
Set a 10 minute prayer time aside where your main focus is to worship God. Don't ask for things.

_____

_____

_____

_____

_____

_____

_____

_____

_____

_____

_____

Week⁴

Introduction

Session 1 –
Leading Yourself:
Finding God's Plan for Your Life

God's Plan for Humanity
God's Plan for Your Life

Break

Session 2 –
Living with Purpose

Setting Personal Goals
Managing Time and Resources

Session 3 –
Managing Myself to Live a Purpose-Driven Life

Homework –
My Personal Development Plan
SOAP Journal

Session 1

Leading Yourself:
Finding God's Plan for Your Life

Outcomes

By the end of this session, you will be able to:

* Identify the overall plan for humanity within history
* Understand that God has a plan for their life
* Understand how that plan connects to the cause of Christ
* Go through the process of finding, framing and articulating that plan

God's Plan for Humanity

God's Plan for Your Life

Session 2
Living with Purpose

Outcomes

By the end of this session, you will be able to:
* Appreciate the need to live a life focused on God-given purpose
* Employ mindset and practices needed to live a focused life (e.g. Goal-setting, time management, debriefs, rest, balance, etc)
* Have identified personal strengths and weaknesses in living a focused life

Setting Personal Goals

Managing Time and Resources

Session 3
Managing Myself to Live a Purpose-Driven Life

In order to live a life that fulfils God's purpose for our lives we need to learn to manage ourselves. Make a list of the things that you consider to be important in your life. Prioritise items according to their importance. Leave the 'Actual Ranking' column for the moment.

What is important to me?

Items	Ranking	Actual Ranking

How do I use my time?

Determine how you spend your typical 24-hour day (see chart on next page). Enter the hours you spend on each activity. Add in to the list any other activity that you do on a typical day. Use Table C to help map your hours.

Activities	No. of Hours
Praying/Devotions	
Studying/School	
Work	
Exercise and sports	
Family commitments	
Eating including preparation & clean up	
Personal grooming	
Relaxing	
Travel	
Socialising/Entertaining	
Sleeping	
Church commitments	

24 -HOURS

	MONDAY	TUESDAY	WEDNESDAY	THURSDAY	FRIDAY	SATURDAY	SUNDAY
12.00AM							
12.30AM							
1.00AM							
1.30AM							
2.00AM							
2.30AM							
3.00AM							
3.30AM							
4.00AM							
4.30AM							
5.00AM							
5.30AM							
6.00AM							
6.30AM							
7.00AM							
7.30AM							
8.00AM							

	MONDAY	TUESDAY	WEDNESDAY	THURSDAY	FRIDAY	SATURDAY	SUNDAY
8.30AM							
9.00AM							
9.30AM							
10.00AM							
10.30AM							
11.00AM							
11.30AM							
12.00PM							
12.30PM							
1.00PM							
1.30PM							
2.00PM							
2.30PM							
3.00PM							
3.30PM							
4.00PM							
4.30PM							
5.00PM							

	MONDAY	TUESDAY	WEDNESDAY	THURSDAY	FRIDAY	SATURDAY	SUNDAY
5.30PM							
4.30PM							
5.00PM							
5.30PM							
6.00PM							
6.30PM							
7.00PM							
7.30PM							
8.00PM							
8.30PM							
9.00PM							
9.30PM							
10.00PM							
10.30PM							
11.00PM							
11.30PM							

On a typical day such as Monday, how much time are you really investing on the things that you consider to be most important to you?

_____

_____

_____

_____

_____

_____

_____

_____

Rank your answers in the 3rd column of the 'What is important to me' table based on the result of your answers in the 'How do I use my time' table. What are your non-negotiables?

_____

_____

_____

_____

_____

_____

_____

What changes do you need to make, to make your 24-hour day reflect the things that are really important to you?

_____

_____

_____

_____

_____

_____

_____

_____

_____

_____

_____

_____

Homework

My Personal Development Plan

Finding God's plan for You

What is God's plan and purpose for your life? What has He called you to be?

_____

_____

_____

_____

_____

_____

_____

_____

_____

_____

_____

_____

_____

_____

_____

_____

_____

_____

_____

_____

_____

_____

_____

_____

_____

_____

_____

_____

If you are still in the process of identifying God's plan for your life, ask yourself the following questions: What do you believe God is saying to you about His plans and purpose for your life?

_____

_____

_____

_____

_____

_____

_____

_____

_____

_____

_____

Ask God to give you a revelation of what He wants you to do. Reflect on the key scriptures that God has given you. What are my gifts, talents and skills? Gifts indicate what God might like us to do with our lives.

_____

_____

_____

_____

_____

_____

_____

_____

_____

_____

_____

What are your strengths and weaknesses or areas for improvement?

Think of specific situations when you observed these gifts, talents, skills, strengths and weaknesses.

_____

_____

_____

_____

_____

_____

_____

_____

_____

_____

_____

_____

_____

_____

_____

_____

_____

_____

_____

_____

_____

_____

_____

_____

_____

_____

_____

What does my family and friends see as my gifts and discern is my calling? What do they see as my strengths and weaknesses or areas for improvement?

If you don't know what they see in you, go and ask them. Ask family & friends who are spiritually mature.

_____

_____

_____

_____

_____

_____

_____

_____

_____

_____

_____

_____

_____

_____

_____

_____

_____

_____

_____

_____

_____

_____

_____

_____

Setting goals and strategies to meeting my goals

Articulate one spiritual and one life goal that you will be willing to commit to accomplish in the next six months. Your life goal could be about family, career, finance, church and community involvement, etc. As a guide, good goals are SMART, meaning they are Specific, Measurable, Attainable, Relevant (to your life mission and interests), and Time-Bound.

My spiritual goal is: _____

My strategies in meeting my spiritual goal are:

_____

_____

_____

_____

_____

_____

_____

_____

_____

_____

_____

_____

I know that I have achieved my spiritual goal, if at the end of six months the following are evident in my life:

_____

_____

_____

_____

_____

_____

_____

_____

_____

My life goal is: _____

My strategies for achieving my life goal are:

_____

_____

_____

_____

_____

_____

_____

_____

_____

_____

_____

_____

_____

I know that I have achieved my life goal, if at the end of six months the following are evident in my life:

_____

_____

_____

_____

_____

_____

_____

_____

_____

_____

_____

_____

SOAP Journal

For this week, pick a passage on worship or faith and reflect on it. Always ask the Holy Spirit to give you insight and to open the Word to you.

Read: _____

Which particular passage did I find striking?

_____

_____

_____

_____

_____

_____

_____

What is the Lord saying to me in this passage with regard to my life?

_____

_____

_____

_____

_____

_____

_____

_____

_____

_____

_____

_____

How does this passage apply to my particular need?

_____

_____

_____

_____

_____

_____

_____

_____

How will I respond to what God has revealed to me?

_____

_____

_____

_____

_____

_____

_____

_____

_____

My prayer:

_____

_____

_____

_____

_____

_____

_____

_____

_____

Week⁵

Introduction

Session 1 –
Leading Yourself: Values and Beliefs

Values
Beliefs

Break

Session 2 –
Leading Yourself: Wisdom

Definitions of Wisdom
The Wisdom of God
The Benefits and Results of Wisdom in our Lives
Developing Wisdom

Session 3 –
My Personal Values

Homework –
Linking My Personal Values to those of My Church
SOAP Journal

Session 1
Leading Yourself: Values and Beliefs

Outcomes

By the end of this session, you will be able to:
* Define their personal values and explain what they mean by them
* Recognise how their values and beliefs affect how they behave and make decisions in life
* Connect their personal values to those of the church
* Demonstrate their values in a consistent manner

Values

Beliefs

Session 2
Leading Yourself: Wisdom

Outcomes

By the end of this session, you will be able to:
* Describe what is meant by godly wisdom
* Differentiate between godly and human wisdom
* Outline the benefits of wisdom for their personal lives
* Understand and apply how to develop wisdom in their own lives

Definition of Wisdom

The Wisdom of God

The Benefits and Results of Wisdom in Our Lives

Developing Wisdom

Session 3
My Personal Values

Identifying our personal values is important because they affect our attitudes and behaviours. This exercise is designed to help you reach a better understanding of your most significant values. We have provided you with a list of common personal values, which is by no means exhaustive, to help you in the process.

Choose ten (10) values that are most important to you, the values you believe in and that define your character. Remember, values are beliefs, ideals or principles that you consider important or find worthwhile. Feel free to add any values of your own to the list.

Acceptance	Faith in God	Competition	Hope
Efficiency	Kindness	Goodness	Practicality
Individuality	Self-Control	Optimism	Wealth
Quality	Change	Success	Dignity
Accomplishment	Flexibility	Contentment	Humility
Empathy	Leadership	Goodwill	Prosperity
Influence	Service	Peace	Wisdom
Relationship	Cleanliness and	Talent	Discipline
Accountability	orderliness	Cooperation	Humour
Empowerment	Following tradition	Gratitude	Purity
Initiative	Learning	Perfection	Working hard
Reliability	Significance	Teamwork	Diversity
Accuracy	Collaboration	Courage	Independence
Enjoyment/Fun	Freedom	Harmony	Purpose
Innocence	Looking good	Perseverance	
Reputation	Simplicity	Thankfulness	
Adventure	Commitment	Creativity	
Equality	Friendliness	Having authority	
Innovativeness	Love	Persistency	
Respect	Sophistication	Time	
Affection	Communication	Credibility	
Ethical practice	Friendship	Health	
Integrity	Loyalty	Physical fitness	
Responsibility	Spontaneity	Tolerance	
Ambition	Compassion	Dedication	
Excellence	Fulfillment	Helping others	
Intelligence	Money	Pleasure	
Righteousness	Standing up for my	Truthfulness	
Beauty	beliefs	Dependability	
Equitable treatment	Competency	Honesty	
Justice	Generosity	Politeness	
Security	Openness	Volunteerism	
Challenge	Stewardship	Devotion	

From the 10 values that you have chosen, select five that you would consider to be very important to you. In choosing your top five, think of specific examples of how each value applies to your life. If you can't think of an example, then the value is probably not a high priority. Then answer the following questions:

How do you demonstrate (in terms of behaviour) these values at home, work and church?

How have your values impacted your relationships with your family and friends?

How would my life be different if my values are prominent and practised?

Homework

**Linking My Personal Values
with the Values of My Local Church**

What are the core values of your local church?

_____

_____

_____

_____

_____

_____

_____

_____

_____

_____

How are these values demonstrated by your local church? Give examples.

_____

_____

_____

_____

_____

_____

_____

_____

_____

_____

_____

How do you demonstrate the values of your local church in your personal life?

_____

_____

_____

_____

_____

_____

_____

_____

_____

_____

_____

In what ways do your values align with or diverge from the values of your local church? If they diverge, what steps will you take to change your values so they line up with those of your local church?

_____

_____

_____

_____

_____

_____

_____

_____

_____

_____

_____

_____

_____

SOAP Journal

For this week, pick a passage you want to read and reflect on. Always ask the Holy Spirit to give you insight and to open the Word to you.

Read: _____

Which particular passage did I find striking?

_____

_____

_____

_____

_____

_____

_____

What is the Lord saying to me in this passage with regard to my life?

_____

_____

_____

_____

_____

_____

_____

_____

_____

_____

_____

_____

_____

_____

_____

How does this passage apply to my particular need?

_____

_____

_____

_____

_____

_____

_____

How will I respond to what God has revealed to me?

_____

_____

_____

_____

_____

_____

_____

My prayer:

_____

_____

_____

_____

_____

_____

_____

_____

_____

Week⁶

Introduction

**Session 1 –
Leading Yourself: Character**

What is Character
Biblical Character Qualities
Developing Christian Character

Break

**Session 2 –
Life with Others: Loving People**

The Importance of Love
The Practice of Love

**Session 3 –
What Does it mean to Love People?**

**Homework –
Developing My Character
SOAP Journal**

Session 1
Leading Yourself: Character

Outcomes

By the end of this session, you will be able to:
* Define character
* Describe the various character qualities that a Christian should seek to develop
* Employ strategies for building character

What is Character?

_____

_____

_____

_____

_____

_____

_____

_____

_____

_____

_____

_____

_____

_____

_____

_____

_____

_____

_____

_____

_____

_____

_____

Biblical Character Qualities

Developing Christian Character

Session 2
Life with Others: Loving People

Outcomes

By the end of this session, you will be able to:
* Define and describe the biblical teaching on love
* Explain the importance of loving people
* Have identified ways they can love others

The Importance of Love

The Practice of Love

Session 3
What does it mean to love people?

"What is written in the Law?" he replied. "How do you read it?" He answered, "'Love the Lord your God with all your heart and with all your soul and with all your strength and with all your mind'; and, 'Love your neighbor as yourself.'" "You have answered correctly," Jesus replied. "Do this and you will live." (Luke 10:26-28)

In its context this passage is part of the story of the Good Samaritan, and is a lesson in what it means to really love all people.

William Barclay, in his commentary on this passage, talks about the Jewish understanding of loving your neighbour. Jesus challenges the expert in the Law to look at the phylactery that he would have been wearing around his wrist – a reminder of the Law – and to think beyond a Jewish definition of neighbour (other Jews) to consider the breadth of who his neighbour might in fact be.

Read Luke 10:25-37 Reflect on the following questions and then discuss with your small group.

Think about how you could re-tell this parable for a 21st century setting? Who would be the equivalent of the Samaritan? Who would be the equivalent of the religious leaders who passed by?

_____

_____

_____

_____

_____

_____

_____

_____

_____

_____

_____

_____

_____

_____

_____

_____

Do we have a similar mindset to the expert in the Law? Are there certain people groups who we have no problem reaching out to, while others that we would not be so quick to reach out to?

_____

_____

_____

_____

_____

_____

_____

_____

_____

_____

Think about ways you could be more inclusive to people you may not previously have reached out to?

_____

_____

_____

_____

_____

_____

_____

_____

_____

_____

_____

_____

_____

Read John 15:13. In your own words, give a one or two sentence definition of this passage.

_____

_____

_____

_____

_____

_____

_____

_____

_____

_____

List five ways you can apply this idea of loving people over the upcoming weeks.

_____

_____

_____

_____

_____

_____

_____

_____

_____

_____

_____

_____

_____

Homework

Developing My Character

Read Genesis 1:26. The scripture tells us that we have been made in the image and likeness of God. The word 'image' does not refer to physical likeness but rather to the nature, characteristics, and essence of God.

Some of the Common Character Traits or Qualities:

Alertness	Honour
Attentiveness	Hospitality
Availability	Humility
Benevolence	Initiative
Boldness	Integrity
Cautiousness	Joyfulness
Cleanliness	Justice
Compassion	Loving
Contentment	Lowly
Courage	Loyalty
Creativity	Meekness
Decisiveness	Obedience
Deference	Orderliness
Dependability	Patience
Determination	Persuasiveness
Diligence	Prudent
Discernment	Punctuality
Discretion	Resourcefulness
Endurance	Responsibility
Enthusiasm	Security
Faith	Self-Control
Faithful	Sensitivity
Fearing God	Sincerity
Flexibility	Steadfast
Forgiveness	Thoroughness
Frugality	Thriftiness
Generosity	Tolerance
Gentleness	Truthfulness
Gratefulness	Virtue
Holy	Wisdom

What character qualities do you believe are already evident in your life? Can you think of specific situations or circumstances when you have displayed these character qualities?

_____

_____

_____

_____

_____

_____

_____

_____

_____

_____

_____

What has been the result or consequences of having these qualities evident in your life?

_____

_____

_____

_____

_____

_____

_____

_____

_____

_____

_____

_____

_____

What character qualities do you feel you need to better develop in your life? Choose at least three qualities that you will be willing to commit to start developing this year.

_____

_____

_____

_____

_____

_____

_____

_____

_____

_____

_____

_____

_____

_____

_____

_____

_____

_____

_____

_____

_____

_____

_____

_____

_____

_____

_____

Putting it into practice

Try to learn more about the character qualities that you have selected. Find someone who already demonstrates those qualities in their lives and talk about them.

_____

_____

_____

_____

_____

_____

_____

_____

_____

_____

_____

_____

_____

_____

_____

_____

_____

_____

_____

_____

_____

_____

Pick one character trait that you want to work on consistently for the day, week or month. As you put them into practice, ask God to give you opportunities to develop those traits. Take time to reflect on your progress. Don't be discouraged with yourself if you find yourself failing along the way. Character is developed by habits and habits are developed by doing something consistently.

SOAP Journal

For this week, pick a passage you want to read and reflect on. Always ask the Holy Spirit to give you insight and to open the Word to you.

Read: _____

Which particular passage did I find striking?

_____

_____

_____

_____

_____

_____

What is the Lord saying to me in this passage with regard to my life?

_____

_____

_____

_____

_____

_____

_____

_____

_____

_____

_____

_____

_____

_____

_____

How does this passage apply to my particular need?

_____

_____

_____

_____

_____

_____

_____

How will I respond to what God has revealed to me?

_____

_____

_____

_____

_____

_____

_____

My prayer:

_____

_____

_____

_____

_____

_____

_____

_____

_____

_____

Week⁷

Introduction

**Session 1 –
Building Relationships**

God's Plan for Relationships
The Importance of Relationships
Keys to Building Great Relationships
Choosing Friends to Your Destiny

Break

**Session 2 –
Relating to the Unsaved**

Sayings that Can Stop Us from Sharing Jesus
A Lesson from Jesus

**Session 3 –
My Relationship Map**

Session 1
Building Relationships

Outcomes

By the end of this session, you will be able to:
* Outline God's plan for relationships
* Explain the importance of relationships
* List and explain important keys to building relationships
* Understand the importance of choosing friends in fulfilling one's destiny
* Identify the qualities needed in such a person
* Evaluate current and potential relationships

God's Plan for Relationships

_____

_____

_____

_____

_____

_____

_____

_____

_____

_____

_____

_____

_____

_____

_____

_____

_____

_____

_____

_____

_____

_____

_____

_____

_____

_____

The Importance of Building Relationships

_____

_____

_____

_____

_____

_____

_____

_____

_____

_____

_____

_____

_____

_____

_____

_____

_____

_____

_____

_____

_____

_____

_____

_____

_____

_____

_____

_____

Keys to Building Great Relationships

Choosing Friends to Your Destiny

Session 2
Relating to the Unsaved

Outcomes

By the end of this session, you will be able to:
* Recognise unhelpful ways of thinking about evangelism
* Initiate conversations with unsaved people
* Relate in a natural and loving manner in their relationships with unsaved people
* Share their testimony

Sayings That Can Stop Us From Sharing Jesus

Session 3
My Relationship Map

Who are the people in your life that you relate to most often?

_____

_____

_____

_____

_____

_____

_____

_____

_____

_____

_____

_____

_____

_____

_____

_____

_____

_____

_____

_____

_____

_____

_____

Categorise the relationships with the people listed above based on your closeness to them.

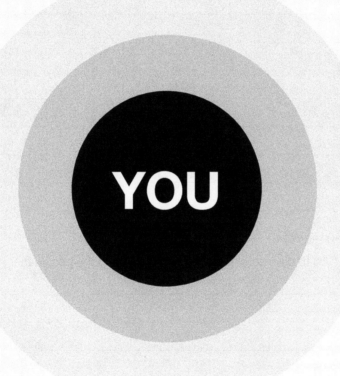

On a scale of 1 to 10, how would you rate the health of your relationship with the people that you have identified? Where would you like to be on the scale by the end of the year? Draw an arrow to show which direction you want to head in.

```
|··············|··············|··············|··············|··············|··············|··············|··············|··············|
1              2              3              4              5              6              7              8              9            10
```

_____

_____

_____

_____

_____

_____

_____

_____

_____

What do you need to do to develop a healthier relationship with the people that you have identified?

_____

_____

_____

_____

_____

_____

_____

_____

_____

_____

_____

_____

To enlarge your circle of friends, you need to develop new ones! Think of someone new that you will commit to becoming a friend with (i.e. neighbour, unsaved workmate, the parent of your child's friend, etc). When will you do it? How will you initiate the friendship?

SOAP Journal

For this week, pick a passage you want to read and reflect on. Always ask the Holy Spirit to give you insight and to open the Word to you.

Read: _____

Which particular passage did I find striking?

_____

_____

_____

_____

_____

_____

_____

What is the Lord saying to me in this passage with regard to my life?

_____

_____

_____

_____

_____

_____

_____

_____

_____

_____

_____

_____

_____

How does this passage apply to my particular need?

_____

_____

_____

_____

_____

_____

_____

How will I respond to what God has revealed to me?

_____

_____

_____

_____

_____

_____

_____

_____

My prayer:

_____

_____

_____

_____

_____

_____

_____

_____

_____

_____

CPSIA information can be obtained
at www.ICGtesting.com
Printed in the USA
BVHW010059260921
617490BV00007B/98